Elizabeth II
Forty Glorious Years

Elizabeth II
Forty Glorious Years

Helene McGowan

Crescent Books
New York

PAGE 1 A stunning
portrait of Queen
Elizabeth's Coronation by
Cecil Beaton.

PAGE 2 A formal portrait
of the Queen.

BELOW Princess Elizabeth
sitting in Queen
Alexandra's French chaise
with two dogs at Windsor
Castle, 30 May 1944.

This 1992 edition published by Crescent Books,
distributed by Outlet Book Company, Inc.,
a Random House Company,
225 Park Avenue South,
New York, New York 10003.

Produced by
Brompton Books Corporation
15 Sherwood Place
Greenwich, CT 06830

ISBN 0-517-06985-7

8 7 6 5 4 3 2 1

Printed and bound in Hong Kong

CONTENTS

A SECLUDED CHILDHOOD

When Princess Elizabeth, daughter of the Duke and Duchess of York, was born at 2.40 am on 21 April 1926, no one present could have known that they had witnessed the birth of the future Queen Elizabeth II of Great Britain and the Commonwealth. Her paternal grandparents King George V and Queen Mary were delighted at the good news. They had asked to be informed immediately and went up to Windsor to see the new baby as soon as they could. Many thought the baby had the look of her venerable grandmother, who leaned over the princess's crib to whisper 'I wish you were more like your little mother.'

The Duchess of York's confinement had taken place at 17 Bruton Street, the London home of her parents, the Earl and Countess of Strathmore. A large crowd of well-wishers had gathered outside the Mayfair mansion. Albert (or Bertie to his friends and family), Duke of York was quite overwhelmed to be a father for the first time. 'You don't know what a tremendous joy it is to Elizabeth and me to have our little girl,' he wrote to his mother, 'We always wanted a child to make our happiness complete, and now that it has happened, it seems so wonderful and strange.' The baby princess was christened in the private chapel at Buckingham Palace on 29 May 1926, when she was five weeks old. She was dressed in the cream Brussels lace gown worn by all royal children since those of her great-great-grandmother Queen Victoria. She was christened Elizabeth Alexandra Mary – all three names remindful of great British queens.

Princess Elizabeth was a very pretty baby with fair hair, tiny ears, long black lashes and light-blue eyes. Everyone thought her adorable and none more so than her paternal grandparents, who doted on her from the very first. The normally shy, reticent Queen Mary thought her a 'little darling' and to the King she became 'dear little Lilibet' (the little girl's lisped attempt at her own name). The Duchess of York's sister

RIGHT An idyllic portrait of the two young Royal Princesses taken by Marcus Adams. Their dresses were often copied by parents who wanted their own daughters to reflect the royal image.

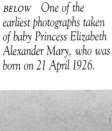

BELOW One of the earliest photographs taken of baby Princess Elizabeth Alexander Mary, who was born on 21 April 1926.

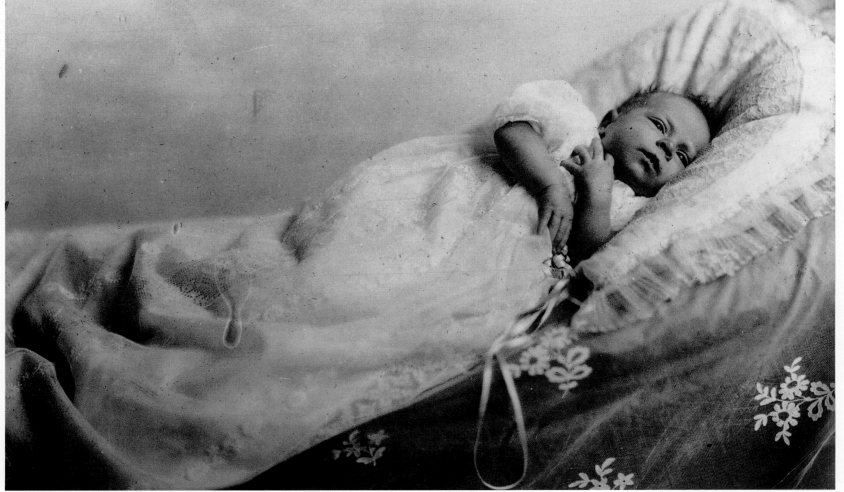

Lady Elphinstone graciously gave up her children's nursemaid Clara Knight to look after the little princess. Clara was known by the courtesy title of Mrs Knight and as Alla to her charges, and had been the Duchess of York's nanny. Old-fashioned and utterly dedicated to her charges, she was a very loyal servant and faithful family retainer to the Strathmore family. Royal legend had it that she was so conscientious that she refused even to take a vacation. In fact, she took a holiday once every year.

When Princess Elizabeth was born her parents were living in White Lodge, a totally unsuitable royal residence, given to them upon their marriage by the King. It was set in the lovely grounds of Richmond Park but was too big, too far from London and too accessible to the public. But it remained their home (with the Bruton Street residence as a more convenient house to use when they were up in London), until they moved into 145 Piccadilly in 1928. The family into which Princess Elizabeth was born was dominated by her grandfather King George V, patriarch to the Windsors and the nation at large. George V took his role as head of the family very seriously indeed. Industry, honour, loyalty and duty were the key to his character and his reign. Not an intellectual, George V was a rather shy and conservative man, who set the ideal of British monarchy that continues to this day. A firm believer in the strengths of constitutional monarchy, he saw his role as one of representation and reflected all the qualities that the British people most admired – steadfastness, commonsense, hard work, dignity and loyalty. The Prince of Wales (later Edward VIII), summed up his father's creed as belief in 'God, in the invincibility of the Royal Navy and the essential rightness of whatever was British.'

The King was happiest living the life of a country squire, which he loved to do at Sandringham, the royal family's country residence in Norfolk. Beneath the gruff, irascible, at times intimidating exterior, he was essentially a highly strung, emotionally repressed man. He could suddenly burst into short-lived, unholy rages. His sons found him a difficult, remote figure when they were children as he was either acting the part of the severe patriarch or teasing them awkwardly. His treatment of them when they were young was always governed by his sense of duty to bring them up as guardians of the throne. George V was always immaculately dressed, with neatly pressed trousers, shined buttons and a white gardenia in the buttonhole of his frock coat. He abhorred sloppiness in others and would not hesitate to correct anyone not measuring up to his sartorial standards.

However, the King was certainly not devoid of some endearing eccentricities; he insisted that all the clocks at Sandringham be set half an hour early at all times and owned a pink and grey parrot who sat on his shoulder and accompanied him into

8

ABOVE The Duchess of York, later Queen Elizabeth, Consort to King George VI, looks down upon her new baby daughter who would one day become Queen Elizabeth II.

RIGHT This photograph shows the devoted nursery maid Clara Knight with the one-year-old Princess Elizabeth driving home from Windsor where they had visited the Queen in March 1927.

BELOW The official royal family group photograph taken at Buckingham Palace after the christening of Princess Elizabeth on 29 May 1926. Standing from left are: the Duke of Connaught, King George V, Prince Albert (the Duke of York), and the Earl of Strathmore. Seated: Lady Elphinstone, Queen Mary, the Duchess of York with Princess Elizabeth, her mother the Countess of Strathmore, and Princess Mary, the Viscountess Lascelles.

BELOW Another charming Marcus Adams' portrait of Princess Elizabeth.

breakfast every morning. As a young child Princess Elizabeth called the King 'Grandpa England' and this child's view of George V epitomizes the simplicity of his identity in the minds of his subjects. He was a very decisive influence on the princess for the first ten years of her life and, as Queen, she has continued his tradition of monarchy in her love of the ordinary, her capacity for hard work, and her dedication to simple family life.

Princess Elizabeth was only nine months old when her parents left Great Britain in January 1927 for a Commonwealth tour of Australia and New Zealand. It was a very testing royal visit, for many in Australia were disappointed that Edward, Prince of Wales, would not be coming over to open the House of Parliament in the newly appointed capital Canberra. The older Prince had made a tour of Australia in 1920 to great public acclaim and adoration. Stanley Bruce, the Australian Prime Minister, openly expressed his doubts about Prince Albert's ability. Bertie stammered as a child and still spoke with difficulty in public, but with the help of Lionel Logue, a Harley Street speech therapist, he made good progress towards conquering his stammer in the months before the departure for Australia. Everyone was pleased when the tour

RIGHT: Hand-in-hand with 'Alla', the three-year-old Princess Elizabeth arrives in Grosvenor Square for a friend's birthday party in July 1929.

12

ABOVE Princess Elizabeth playing with the children of Princess Mary, whose friendship with Lady Elizabeth Bowes-Lyon (the Duchess of York before her marriage to the Duke) was instrumental in the courtship of The Duke of York and Elizabeth.

proved a success. While her parents were abroad Princess Elizabeth was shared between her two sets of grandparents – the Strathmores at their country home of St Paul's Waldenbury in Herefordshire, and the King and Queen at Buckingham Palace. She was sent to stay at the palace from the end of February onwards. 'Our sweet little granddaughter Elizabeth arrived today,' wrote the King in his diary, 'and came to see us after tea.' It was the baby's first prolonged contact with her grandmother, Queen Mary. Princess Elizabeth was a mere fourteen months old when she appeared on the balcony of Buckingham Palace for the first time on 27 June 1927 as part of the homecoming celebrations on the return of her parents from their long tour.

In November 1928 the King fell seriously ill and at one stage was close to death. He was suffering from bronchial pneumonia, toxaemia and blood poisoning but his will to live was strong and with the best medical care available he pulled through. The King was sent to Bognor to recuperate and in March 1929 Princess Elizabeth joined him there – she was the best possible tonic for her adoring grandfather. The two would sit and play together in the sandpit and every afternoon the little girl could be seen trotting beside his Bath chair while the King went out for his daily constitutional. It was clear to any observer that a close, affectionate bond was already well established. Lady Airlie, Queen Mary's lady-in-waiting remarked: 'He used to play – a thing I never saw him do with his own children'.

Upon their return from their Commonwealth tour, the Yorks moved into the first proper home of their own – 145 Piccadilly – a large, rented crown property across Green Park from Buckingham Palace. It was elegant and spacious with a sunny nursery right at the top of the house. On 21 August 1930 Princess Elizabeth ceased being an only child when her mother gave birth to a second daughter during a fierce rain storm. The baby was born at her mother's ancestral home in Scotland, Glamis Castle, thus reaffirming the royal family's Scottish connections. The Yorks wished to call their daughter Margaret Anne but George V had very obstinate ideas about names for royal babies (he had not been too happy with the choice of Elizabeth initially) and he did not want an Anne in the family. So her parents settled on the name Margaret Rose. Princess Elizabeth decided her sister should be called Bud. 'I've got a baby sister Margaret Rose' she informed Lady Cynthia Asquith, 'and I'm going to call her Bud.' When asked why, the four-and-a-half-year-old girl replied with unerring logic, 'Well, she's not a real Rose yet, is she?'

It was partly out of gratitude for a new granddaughter that George V presented the Yorks with a country residence, Royal Lodge, a Georgian-cum-Regency mansion in Windsor Great Park. Once a palatial residence and private retreat of the Prince Regent, the house was now in ruins. Elizabeth and Bertie went to see the property in September 1931 and fell in love with it. After extensive renovations which included having the exterior painted rose pink and the gardens planted and redesigned (partly by the Yorks themselves), the Duke and Duchess and their daughters moved in during January 1932. Royal Lodge became a very special weekend home and private retreat for the young family.

RIGHT The young Princess out for a ride on her tricycle.

RIGHT A serious-looking Princess Elizabeth dutifully holds her sister Princess Margaret Rose's hand at a fancy-dress party at the London home of Lady Astor in February 1934.

In 1933 a 23-year-old nursery governess, Marion Crawford, was engaged at 145 Piccadilly for a three-month trial period and stayed for 17 years. She had trained at Edinburgh's Moray House and was a go-ahead progressive governess. She had originally intended to return to college to become a child psychologist. When her book *The Little Princesses* was published in the 1950s the royal family were greatly upset by what they saw as a grave betrayal of trust. 'Crawfie,' as she was known to the two princesses, wrote that she was pleasantly surprised to see the princesses were not the 'spoiled and difficult little people' that she had been expecting. Miss Crawford was tall and slim with a short, very stylish, Eton crop hair-do and her own ideas about child rearing. Clashes between her and the equally strong-minded Alla were not uncommon. The other principal servant in the young Elizabeth's life was 'Bobo' Margaret MacDonald, a sensible Scottish lass from Inverness who was a devoted nursery maid and friend to the young princess. She later became Princess Elizabeth's personal maid and dresser and lifelong friend.

Princess Elizabeth was a very well-behaved, dutiful, polite child. She was no trouble to teach or to dress whereas her sister Margaret was a little more self-willed: one of her earliest memories is of deliberately falling out of her pram to gain attention. Margaret's wit and quick tongue were in evidence from an early age. 'You don't look very angelic, Margaret!' said her mother one day as Princess Margaret was about to leave for a fancy-dress party. 'That's all right,' answered Margaret with aplomb, 'I'll be a holy terror.' Margaret, remembered Crawfie in her book, was a 'born comic' and once made her governess laugh by asking her 'Have you ever tried putting toothpaste back into the tube?' Princess Elizabeth was very concerned with neatness and orderliness; she was always systematic and her belongings were always carefully arranged.

When it was decided that Princess Elizabeth was old enough to have an organized school timetable, Crawfie drew up one which consisted of mornings filled with half-hour lessons, and afternoons given over to singing, music and dancing. At Queen Mary's behest, the schedule was modified to include more history and geography.

RIGHT The Yorks and family with pet dogs are pictured in their golden pre-abdication days of June 1936. 'Y Bwthyn Bach' is a beautiful miniature cottage, presented to Princess Elizabeth in 1931.

14

BELOW The Duchess of York, Princess Margaret, Princess Elizabeth, and canine friend arrive for a holiday in Scotland at Glamis Castle, the ancestral home of the Strathmore family.

ABOVE Princess Elizabeth with her favourite Uncle, David, Prince of Wales, ride together on the way back from church at Balmoral, Scotland during the royal family's annual holiday there in February 1933.

RIGHT Balmoral, the Queen's official Scottish residence and a place of seclusion and peace for Queen Elizabeth II.

16

17

Home was very much at the heart of their life and the girls saw a lot of their parents despite the Yorks' pressing work commitments. However they led a secluded existence; the two girls only mixed with a handful of other children and only those drawn from their own aristocratic circle. Trips into the world outside the royal residences were made only occasionally and mostly confined to visits to the zoo, the Royal Horse Show or the annual outing to a pantomime. Lunch was taken with the Duke and Duchess whenever they were at home and 'David', the Prince of Wales, their very affectionate uncle, often popped in for tea and fun and games before bathtime.

Friday afternoons were special – the whole family would journey down to Royal Lodge for a weekend relaxing in the garden and horse riding in Windsor Great Park. Princess Elizabeth loved her many pets – budgerigars, dogs, horses and ponies. She was just three when George V presented her with her first pony at Christmas. He was keen for her to learn to ride and she has repaid him with her world-renowned skill as a horsewoman. In 1933 the Duke of York had brought the first in a long line of corgis to 145

LEFT *King George V's last journey through London. The streets were crowded with hundreds of thousands of people paying homage to their late King. Here we see the gun carriage passing through Parliament Square on its way to Paddington Station from where it was taken to Windsor for the interment.*

RIGHT *The front cover of an edition of the Tatler from May 1920 featured this photo of the 'Little Prince', seen in Honolulu during a tour of the United States. The Prince of Wales was one of the century's first media heroes.*

Piccadilly. On the whole, it was the Duchess of York's priorities which determined the lives of her daughters; she wanted them to 'spend as long as possible in the open air, to enjoy to the full the pleasures of the country, to be able to dance and to draw and appreciate music, to acquire good manners and perfect deportment, and to cultivate the distinctively feminine graces.'

This charmed, safe 'golden age' of childhood could not last. In 1935 George V celebrated his Silver Jubilee. He was surprised and overwhelmed by the public display of love and gratitude shown to him by his people. 'I'm sure I can't understand it,' he told the Archbishop of Canterbury, 'for after all, I am only a very ordinary fellow.' Public affection soon turned to grief however, when the seventy-year-old King's health suddenly failed him during Christmas of 1935. He was suffering from severe heart and lung problems. The end came suddenly at 11.55 pm on 20 January 1936.

No one was more shocked and surprised at the King's death than his eldest son. The Prince of Wales' grief was deemed 'frantic and unreasonable' and 'far exceeding that of his mother and three brothers' by Major Alexander, soon to be the new King's Private Secretary. In a matter of months the monarchy was enveloped in the most serious crisis it had faced for decades. Only a few weeks after the death of George V, the Prime Minister, Stanley Baldwin, expressed his doubts about Edward VIII's ability to 'stay the course' to Clement Attlee, the Labour leader. The causes of the problem were complicated. 'David' had always presented the most congenial face of royalty. He was good looking, charming, dashing and something of a celebrity with a high public profile. Seen as a man of the people, he was the royal with the common touch, and had won the right to fight in the trenches during World War I. He was the first member of the royal family to speak on the radio and he even featured in popular songs – most famously 'I Danced with a Man Who Danced with a Girl Who Danced with the Prince of Wales.' His reign was hailed as a new age, a move away from the staid worthiness of his parents.

His complicated love life was an open secret in London Society and had long been a source of worry to the King and Queen. He had affairs with several women, by far the most serious of which was with his long-term mistress Freda Dudley Ward, the wife of a Liberal MP. His behaviour greatly irritated his parents and was a source of constant tension within the royal family. His easy-going public image belied his private behaviour; he could be moody, arrogant, and self-indulgent. For all his gaiety and dazzle, he was in need of a strong, constant centre to his life.

In 1930 he met Mrs Wallis Simpson, a twice-divorced member of an impoverished Baltimore family. The Prince of Wales was soon obsessively in love with her. He showered Wallis with jewels, many of which were not his to give away, as they were royal heirlooms, such as the emeralds bequeathed by Queen Alexandra to the Prince of Wales, to be worn by his future wife. This brazen breach of royal protocol greatly upset his parents who found their son's consort quite unsuitable. The Prince was neglecting his duties and grew bored with his public role as he became more and more fascinated by the self-possessed, and very dominant, Mrs Simpson. He saw less of his family, causing a major split in its ranks. Wallis did her best to get the ladies of the family on her side but to no avail. All the important royal wives were against her, none more so than Elizabeth, Duchess of York, who resented her as an interfering, unwelcome outsider. Wallis did not know how to behave in a way that would even begin to endear her to royal circles. By the end of 1935, all the sons of George V were married, except for the Prince of Wales.

The ensuing scandal was only kept out of the newspapers by an informal agreement

19

that meant the Press left the private lives of the adult members of the royal family alone. But this state of affairs could not continue once Fleet Street realized the full potential of the unfolding drama. Meanwhile, the new King was causing his government grave concern. He had developed the unforgivable habit of leaving the royal despatch boxes lying around his home, Fort Belvedere – they were often returned unread and stained with the marks left by cocktail glasses. He strongly disagreed with his senior ministers over their attitude to Hitler and Mussolini, who found to their delight that they had a friend sitting on the throne of England. If Edward VIII had not abdicated, his political leanings may well have caused a constitutional crisis in themselves.

In October 1936 Wallis obtained a divorce from her husband Ernest Simpson and the whole sensational story finally broke in the British Press the following December. The King was shocked to learn that most of the papers were against him and his wish to marry Mrs Simpson. On 10 December 1936 King Edward VIII signed the Instrument of Abdication and it was ratified in Parliament. All talk of Beaverbrook's and Winston Churchill's 'King's party', the possibility of a morganatic marriage, and the public debate over love of one's country versus love of a woman were pointless now.

When Princess Elizabeth heard the news at 145 Piccadilly, she flew up the stairs to tell Princess Margaret, who said 'poor you' when she realized that her elder sister would one day be Queen. Elizabeth was said to be the calmest person in the house that day, filled as it was with comings and goings and solemn, hushed tones. When the 10-year-old princess had been a baby, a perceptive visitor had written that she had 'the sweetest air of complete serenity', and that air of serenity has never deserted her, in grief or in joy. When her grandfather George V bestowed the title of Duke of York on a young Prince Albert, he had written to his son: 'I feel this splendid old title will be safe in your hands, and that you will never do anything which could in any way tarnish it.' It was also the old King's professed hope that 'nothing will come between my beloved Lilibet and the throne.' In the light of his eldest son's abdication his words seem strangely prophetic.

A FUTURE
QUEEN

The Coronation date of 12 May 1937 remained unchanged. George VI gave 11-year-old Princess Elizabeth a specially bound volume of the Coronation service to study. He allowed Margaret, at her insistence, to have a train like her elder sister but it would be a few inches shorter just as she was a few inches shorter than Princess Elizabeth. A specially constructed seat had to be built for Princess Margaret in the coach which bore her to Westminster Abbey so that she was visible. In an unprecedented break with tradition, a first for her, Queen Mary decided that she, the Dowager Queen, would attend the Coronation ceremony as she felt her son needed the support of her presence.

Princess Elizabeth was quite pleased with the conduct of her sister during the service, remarking that 'I only had to nudge her once or twice when she played with the prayer books too loudly.' When Queen Mary stood with the two princesses to acknowledge the cheers of the crowds below Buckingham Palace, their balcony drew even louder cheers than the one which held the new King and Queen. Their grandmother did all she could to instill into the two princesses what it meant to be royal. She liked to take them on cultural tours of London – to the Tower, the Royal Mint, Greenwich Palace, Hampton Court, Kew – and she lectured them on royal heritage and history. The King made sure their education was broadbased and, remembering his stifling schooldays in a dingy, dull schoolroom, he directed that their classroom at Buckingham Palace have a light and cheerful ambiance.

The move from 145 Piccadilly to the Palace was a necessary one, but was made much easier by the Queen's talents as a homemaker. The wide corridors and large, often poorly decorated rooms of Buckingham Palace certainly contrasted with the pleasant intimacy of their old home but the girls adapted very well. In April 1983, during an appearance on Radio Four's 'Desert Island Discs', Princess Margaret recalled that the Palace was: 'a very cosy place. We were put into rooms which are nearly always the nursery, and the Queen's children have been brought up in the same apart-

BELOW Coronation day, 12 May 1937. The royal family gather on a balcony of Buckingham Palace to acknowledge the cheers of the crowd below. The newly-crowned King George VI has a fatherly hand on Princess Margaret's oversized crown, which threatens to slip and end up around her forehead.

RIGHT The new King and Queen pose for an official portrait, released as part of the preparations for the Coronation.

24

ABOVE *The official Coronation Day group photograph of the royal family taken at Buckingham Palace. From left to right: the Princess Royal, the Duchess of Gloucester, the Duke of Gloucester, Queen Mary, King George VI, Queen Elizabeth, the Duke of Kent, the Duchess of Kent, and Her Majesty the Queen of Norway. Princess Elizabeth and Princess Margaret stand side-by-side in front.*

RIGHT *The Duke and Duchess of Windsor avoid the direct gaze of the camera as they pose for photographs after their wedding on 3 June 1937.*

LEFT Marion Crawford accompanies the two Princesses on a visit to the Headquarters of the YWCA off Tottenham Court Road in London, May 1939. The Princesses enjoyed their first-ever ride on the London Underground during the trip.

BELOW Elizabeth the horsewoman on her thirteenth birthday, 21 April 1939, at Windsor Castle. The Queen is an excellent horsewoman and her knowledge of racing, dressage and breeding is respected throughout the equine world.

ments.' Their governess Miss Crawford felt that the princesses had brought the Palace back to life.

Many people had doubts about the new King's ability to please and interest his subjects. Two weeks after the coronation, Stanley Baldwin expressed his doubts to Lady Airlie: 'There's a lot of prejudice against him. He's had no chance to capture the popular imagination as his brother did.' But George VI was not concerned with capturing his peoples' imagination – he simply was not that kind of man. The princesses had brought all the energy and charisma of youth into the royal family, and Queen Elizabeth was there to provide elegance. The King's greatest qualities were his steadfastness and dedication to duty, the very virtues needed to heal the damage the abdication crisis had done to the nation and the monarchy. The King felt it was up to him to 'make amends for what has happened.' He was a very hardworking and conscientious man who read his official papers very carefully and took his own notes after meetings with his ministers. He cared deeply about the welfare of his subjects. 'I found him to be well-informed about all that was taking place,' wrote US President Harry Truman years later after World War II, 'I was impressed with the King as a good man.'

The King had to deal with an angry Duke of Windsor who was annoyed that his wife had not been accorded the title 'Her Royal Highness' to which she had no automatic right. He certainly had no reason to complain financially. He was granted £60,000 a year from the Sovereign's Privy Purse and was paid the sum of one million pounds for the royal estates of Sandringham and Balmoral. He showed great insensitivity in marrying the Duchess on 3 June 1937, his father's birthday. The couple's visit to Nazi Germany later that year included a meeting with Hitler that severely embarrassed the British government and George VI.

On 21 April 1939 Princess Elizabeth turned 13, and to mark this occasion her father arranged for her to begin lessons on the British constitution with Sir Henry Marten, Vice Provost of Eton. She visited him in his study at the college twice a week. The lessons were strongly influenced by the writings of the nineteenth-century historian

ABOVE *Prince Philip looking blond and handsome in a schoolboy production of* Macbeth *(he played Donaldbain), at Gordonstoun, Scotland.*

ABOVE *Queen Mary and the little Princesses, in identical and very fashionable outfits, visit the Royal Tournament at Olympia in May 1939.*

Walter Bagehot. It was at this impressionable age that the princess met her future husband for the first time. As part of the royal family's summer cruise, the *Victoria and Albert* yacht sailed up the river Dart on 22 July 1939 and dropped anchor at the Dartmouth Royal Naval College. George VI had spent an unsuccessful period there from 1908-1912. One of his cadet companions at the college had been Louis 'Dickie' Mountbatten, who now showed the King and Queen around Dartmouth.

Lord Mountbatten's nephew Prince Philip of Greece, as he then was (although he did not have a drop of Greek blood in him), was detailed to look after the two princesses and came aboard the royal yacht later that evening for dinner. Princess Elizabeth was immediately smitten with her handsome, 18-year-old third cousin. Prince Philip was Danish by heritage and looked very much the young Viking with his ash-blonde hair and strong, jutting jawline. World War II was now only months away and it was to dominate their relationship for the next six years. In his official biography of King George VI, a book commissioned and carefully checked by Queen Elizabeth II, Sir John Wheeler Bennet had no doubts about what had occurred that day on 22 July. He wrote of the young Prince Philip that he 'was the man with whom Princess Elizabeth had been in love from their very first meeting.'

When the war broke out on 3 September 1939, the royal family was at Balmoral. The King and Queen immediately returned to London and their daughters were taken to Birkhall, a second royal Scottish residence. 'Who is this Hitler, spoiling everything?' demanded nine-year-old Princess Margaret. The whole family went to Sandringham as usual that Christmas. In February 1940 the princesses moved down to Royal Lodge, and after Dunkirk and the fall of France that summer they went to live in Windsor castle until the end of the war. The princesses were protected at Windsor by a special corps of troops and took shelter in converted cellars until a proper air-raid shelter was built for the royal family. The two girls would walk down to the shelter with their little suitcases containing dolls, a book or two and their most treasured personal knick knacks. By the end of the war 300 high-explosive bombs had landed in Windsor Great Park.

The King and Queen would ring their daughters every evening at 6 pm, and joined them at the weekends when possible. On 12 September 1940 Buckingham Palace was bombed on what was to be the first of many occasions. The Queen was heard to declare: 'I'm glad we've been bombed, it makes me feel I can look the East End in the face.' She and the King had seen enough of the nation's wartime devastation to know how the ordinary people were suffering. That Christmas the King included the line 'Now we are all in the front line' in his broadcast to the people. Although far more fortunate than most, the royal family ate by the ration book and Buckingham Palace was full of cold, draughty rooms with blacked out, boarded-up windows. In September 1942, Eleanor Roosevelt visited England and stayed at the Palace where she was very

RIGHT *A relaxed and smiling Queen Elizabeth and Princess Elizabeth photographed in April 1940 at Royal Lodge, Windsor, the family's very special private retreat.*

28

ABOVE Princess Elizabeth on her thirteenth birthday riding in Windsor Great Park with her father, April 1939.

RIGHT An earnest Princess Elizabeth, with Princess Margaret sitting beside her, makes her first radio broadcast in 1940.

ABOVE RIGHT A reflective Princess Elizabeth, dressed in her Girl Guides Uniform, sits on the grass at Frogmore, Windsor in June 1942.

FAR RIGHT Princess Elizabeth and Princess Margaret spent the duration of the War at Windsor Castle. Here they are performing their Christmas pantomime Aladdin in 1943.

surprised to be given 'meals that might have been served in any home in England'.

When Princess Elizabeth was confirmed on 1 March 1942, Lady Airlie thought she had a regal air that reminded her of Queen Victoria. She described the 15-year-old Elizabeth of that day in some detail:

> I saw a grave little face under a small veil and a slender figure in a plain white woollen frock coat. The carriage of her head was unequalled, and there was about her that indescribable something which Queen Victoria had.

After her confirmation the princess said to a friend, 'I'll have to try to be good, won't I?', and this high-minded seriousness is a hallmark of her character. She and Prince Philip wrote to each other throughout the war and he visited the royal family at Windsor castle when his leave from active service in the Mediterranean allowed. The King and Queen believed the friendship was good for Elizabeth. Philip was a good humoured, well-balanced young man who could bring the realities of the outside world a little closer to the Princess. The King did not really see him as a potential suitor for his eldest daughter, but the Queen, a less possessive parent than her husband, was happy for the friendship to develop further.

Like her father, Princess Elizabeth was frustrated at not being able to play a more direct part in the war, but the King would not let her commence war work until she was 18. In the spring of 1945, Princess Elizabeth was proud to join the Auxiliary Transport Service as: 'No 230873 Second Subaltern Elizabeth Alexandra Mary Windsor. No 1 Mechanical Transport Training Centre, Age: 18. Height: 5 feet 3 inches. Eyes: blue. Hair: brown.' As the war drew to a close, it was clear that Princess Elizabeth and Prince Philip's feelings for one another could no longer be dismissed as mere teenage infatuation. Philip's older cousin, King George of Greece, approached Elizabeth's father to sound him out. 'We think she is too young for that now', replied the King in March 1944, 'as she has never met any young men of her own age. . . . I like Philip. He is intelligent, has a good sense of humour, and thinks about things in the right way.' In other words, the King was saying Philip was not out of the running, but he was going to have to wait.

ABOVE *An informal photograph of the Queen, Princess Elizabeth and Princess Margaret with one of their many pet dogs. The Queen's pretty floral dress is typical of the designs she chose to wear throughout the war. She believed that the British people would benefit far more from seeing her in pastel, feminine frocks than dressed in any kind of uniform, and she was right.*

On 8 May 1945, Britain went wild celebrating the victory in Europe. The King and Queen, the two Princesses and Winston Churchill stood on a balcony at Buckingham Palace to wave to the joyous crowds below them. The King allowed a carefully chosen group of escorts to take the Princesses out into the streets to mingle with the celebrating crowds. George VI was touched that his subjects were grateful that the royal family had stayed and helped the nation throughout the war. Many of the monarchs of other European countries had sought exile abroad but the King and Queen would not entertain such a thought. 'We have been overwhelmed by the kind things people have said over our part in the war', the King wrote in his diary, 'We have only tried to do our duty during these five and a half years.' The King was very sad to have to say goodbye to Winston Churchill as his Prime Minister when the Labour Party swept to victory in the General Election of 1945. The two men had built up a very close, mutually admiring relationship and the King felt that Churchill had been shabbily treated. The Labour leader, Clement Attlee, was a terse, reticent man and there were awkward silences during his first audiences with the King – they were simply too alike to communicate easily. George VI confessed he found some of his new socialist ministers 'rather difficult to talk to.'

In September 1945, the royal family went to Balmoral for a long private holiday. Princess Elizabeth was revealing a stubborn and surprisingly independent streak in her determination to marry Prince Philip. She resisted all her father's attempts to interest her in other suitable young men. In the late summer of 1946, she cast aside the doubts of others and the problems that arose from Philip's background and said yes to his proposal of marriage while he was visiting at Balmoral. The royal family were due to make a tour of South Africa in early 1947 and the King was very keen for them all to go

ABOVE RIGHT *King George VI and his elder daughter pictured at White Lodge, Richmond Park. Their physical resemblance is clear but the Princess also inherited her father's sense of dedication and reserved public demeanour.*

RIGHT *Princess Elizabeth has fun dancing the encore to an eightsome reel at the Royal Caledonian Ball at Grosvenor House, London, June 1946.*

ABOVE At last Princess Elizabeth is able to play a real role in Britain's wartime effort. Here she grins at the camera as she undergoes her vehicle maintenance training in the ATS in April 1945.

together. He asked that the engagement be kept secret and Princess Elizabeth agreed so long as she could marry Philip on her return.

The tour began on 1 February 1947 and while abroad, Princess Elizabeth celebrated her twenty-first birthday. She made a special broadcast to the people of the Commonwealth to honour the occasion. Her theme was duty and her sense of dedication was plainly conveyed: 'I declare to you all,' she said, ' that my whole life, whether it be long or short, shall be devoted to your service and the service of our great Imperial Commonwealth to which we all belong.' Meanwhile, Prince Philip became a naturalized British citizen (and so ceased to be a Prince of Greece), and changed his name to the anglicized version of his mother's name, Mountbatten, from the German version, Battenburg.

The engagement was officially announced from Buckingham Palace on 10 July 1947. 'They both came to see me after luncheon looking radiant,' wrote Queen Mary in her diary. Winston Churchill said the news was a 'flash of colour on the hard road we have to travel'. The House of Commons voted that £50,000 be set aside to redecorate Clarence House for the young couple, a move that met with surprisingly little public criticism considering the austerity of the times and that there were 600 rooms in Buckingham Palace. Norman Hartnell designed the beautiful silk wedding dress Princess Elizabeth wore on 20 November 1947. Winston Churchill's wife Clementine expressed the feelings of many people when she said that the young couple's wedding day was a 'shining miracle'.

The nation had taken this ideal daughter to its hearts when she was a child and people celebrated her wedding day as they would for their own daughter. Princess Elizabeth was dutiful, modest and pretty and had been made to wait an uncomfortably long time for this happiness. The King was deeply moved at the loss of this precious

OPPOSITE, TOP LEFT A delightful photographic study of the Queen and her daughters, taken in 1944.

OPPOSITE, TOP RIGHT Princess Elizabeth looks directly into the camera for this 1944 portrait.

OPPOSITE PAGE, BELOW LEFT The royal family in a famous portrait at Buckingham Palace in May 1942.

OPPOSITE PAGE, BELOW RIGHT: No 230873 Second Subaltern Elizabeth Alexandra Mary Windsor of the ATS stands before her vehicle during her training.

33

member of his immediate family. 'I was so proud of you and thrilled at having you so close to me on our long walk in the Abbey,' he wrote to her, 'but when I handed your hand over to the Archbishop, I felt as though I had lost something very precious. You were so calm and composed during the service and said your words with such conviction.' The newlyweds began their honeymoon at Broadlands, Uncle Dickie's Hampshire home. A few days later the Princess received a letter from her father which ended with the following touching lines:

> Your leaving has left a great blank in our lives but do remember that your old home is still yours and do come back to it as much and as often as possible. I can see that you are sublimely happy with Philip which is right but don't forget us is the wish of
> Your ever loving and devoted Papa

Within three months of her wedding, Princess Elizabeth was pregnant. Prince Charles Philip Arthur George was born at Buckingham Palace on 14 December 1948. Queen Mary wrote that she was 'delighted at being a great grandmother.' Princess Elizabeth was overjoyed to be a mother. 'Don't you think he is quite adorable,' she wrote to a friend, 'I still can't believe he is really mine, but perhaps that happens to all new parents. Anyway, this particular boy's parents couldn't be more pleased with him.' As always, awareness of her public duty and the importance of even this most intimate event to millions of other people accompanied her private feelings: 'It's wonderful to think, isn't it, that his arrival could give a bit of happiness to so many other people, besides ourselves, at this time.'

Philip, awarded the title Duke of Edinburgh on his marriage, did not find it easy to adjust to his new life as a princess's consort. A ceremonial existence walking two steps behind his wife was not one for which his naval training had prepared him. He very

35

LEFT Thousands of well-wishers wave to King George VI and Princess Elizabeth as they ride to the Abbey in the bridal coach. Here the carriage passes the Victoria Memorial on the way from Buckingham Palace to Westminster Abbey.

ABOVE A radiant Princess Elizabeth walks up the aisle of Westminster Abbey with her husband Prince Philip on her wedding day, 20 November 1947.

LEFT The official engagement photograph of Princess Elizabeth and Prince Philip. It is a good deal more formal than the comparable photographs of young royalty that we are used to seeing today.

much wanted to command his own ship and the assumption was that he and Princess Elizabeth would live like any other young naval couple. No one knew that the Princess would inherit the throne within a few short years. November 1948 brought the first indications that all was not well. The King had developed the first signs of the illness that would kill him. Cramps in his legs were diagnosed as arteriosclerosis, an obstruction to the circulation through the veins in his legs. There was a danger of thrombosis, and rest was vital. In spring 1949, an operation was performed to relieve the condition and the King recovered well. That autumn the Duke of Edinburgh took up a posting as First Lieutenant and Second in Command of HMS *Chequers*, leader of the First Mediterranean Destroyer Flotilla. Princess Elizabeth flew out to join him in Malta shortly before Christmas 1949. It was the nearest she had ever come to living a normal life, free of the routines and duties of royal life. She could spend her days shopping, sunbathing and picnicking with the other naval wives. Lord Mountbatten was Flag

ABOVE Prince Philip and his bride pose together after their wedding on a day of national celebration not seen in Britain since the 1930s.

Officer commanding the First Cruiser Squadron in the Mediterranean and he invited the couple to stay at his house, the Villa Guaremangia, overlooking the harbour. By spring 1950 the Princess was pregnant again and she flew back to Clarence House to await the birth of her second child.

Prince Philip joined her in July in time for the arrival of Princess Anne Elizabeth Alice Louise on 15 August 1950. That same morning, Philip heard he had been given a ship of his own, HMS *Magpie*, a frigate in the Mediterranean fleet. He and the Princess enjoyed a second brief respite from royal duties but in July 1951 Philip left the Navy on indefinite leave and has never returned. The reason was that the King was ill again and the news was very bad; he had cancer. He had looked tired and tense when

he opened the Festival of Britain on 3 May 1951. 'The incessant worries and crises through which we have to live have got me down properly,' he had written to a friend. The King was a worrier and as his eldest daughter once said, he 'never thought of himself'. He was never told he was suffering from lung cancer and believed that the operation to remove his left lung in September 1951 was necessary because of a bronchial tube blockage. Princess Elizabeth and her husband delayed their departure for their tour of Canada and the United States until the King's doctors were confident of a good recovery for their patient. They finally left in October 1951 for a 35-day tour of the North American continent, where they were warmly received. The King's health seemed much improved when he posed for photographs with his grandson to mark the little boy's third birthday in November 1951. Prince Charles' only memory of his grandfather is of those moments when they sat side by side on a sofa, while the King's Press Secretary swang something shiny on the end of his watch chain to gain his attention. Today, the photograph hangs on the wall of the Queen's private sitting room. On 21 December the King celebrated his fifty-sixth birthday quietly at home with his family. The royal family went to Sandringham as usual that Christmas.

On 30 January 1952 the King and Queen, Princess Margaret and Princess Elizabeth and her husband went to the Drury Lane Theatre to see 'South Pacific'. It was a treat to celebrate the King's recovery and a send off for his daughter and the Duke of Edinburgh who embarked on an ambitious tour of Australia and New Zealand the next day. On 5 February the King enjoyed a good day's shooting at Sandringham. He passed away sometime in the early hours of the next morning and was discovered dead by his valet who came to wake him as usual. He had died in the royal home he had loved best and where he had been born.

Elizabeth and Philip were in Kenya on the first leg of their tour. The new Queen spent her last days as a Princess at Treetops, a hut built into the branches of a giant fig tree, overlooking a waterhole, situated in the Aberdare Forest Game Reserve which was given to the Princess as a present from the people of Kenya at the time of her marriage. The Duke of Edinburgh's Private Secretary Sir Michael Parker informed him of the news from England. 'He looked as if you'd dropped half the world on him,' Parker later recalled, 'I never felt so sorry for anyone in all of my life.' It was 2.45 pm local time, 11.45 am in London when the Duke took his wife for a walk along the banks of the Sangara River to tell her that her beloved father was dead and that at 25 years old, she was now Queen of Great Britain and the Commonwealth.

ACCESSION TO THE THRONE

When the new Queen landed at London Airport, three Prime Ministers past, present and future, were there to greet her – Clement Attlee, Winston Churchill and Anthony Eden. They bowed their heads in homage to their Sovereign as she walked down the airplane steps, alone and in black. Anthony Eden wrote in 1960: 'The sight of that young figure in black coming through the doors of the aircraft, standing there poised for a second before descending . . . is a poignant memory.' Lord Mountbatten's daughter Pamela was a member of the royal entourage on the aborted tour of the Commonwealth and was at Treetops when the news of the King's death reached the Queen. 'Her return was terrible,' she wrote later, 'it was a double grief. She was stunned.'

All those who witnessed the new Queen at this time were struck by her equanimity – she even drafted the apologies to Australia and New Zealand herself. At 4 pm on 7 February 1952 the Queen was back at Clarence House. Queen Mary arrived from Marlborough House and insisted on greeting her granddaughter in the traditional manner. 'Her old Grannie and subject,' she said, 'must be the first to kiss her hand.' Over 330,000 mourners queued to file past the King's coffin of Sandringham oak as it

BELOW: Princess Elizabeth and Prince Philip with baby Charles in 1949.

RIGHT: Cecil Beaton's evocative portrait of Queen Elizabeth II on her coronation.

42

43

lay in state in Westminster Hall. The entire country observed two minutes silence when the coffin was lowered into the ground at St George's Chapel Windsor on 15 February 1952.

The evening before the burial the King's elder daughter had stood quietly in the shadows of a doorway as the mourners and strangers filed past her father's coffin. George VI was uppermost in the Queen's mind when she made her accession declaration: 'My heart is too full,' she told the nation, 'for me to say anything to you today other than that I shall always work as my father did.' Queen Mary felt too weak to attend the funeral; George VI was the third of her sons she had mourned. She was aware that it would not be long before others would be mourning her. She was as indomitable as ever, telling a friend over dinner, 'I'm losing my memory but I mean to get it back.' When she died on 31 March 1953, she was at peace, knowing the throne was safe in the hands of her precious granddaughter.

On 2 June 1953, the entire population of the Commonwealth celebrated the Coronation of Queen Elizabeth II. The United Kingdom indulged in a huge, nationwide jamboree of street parties, and every kind of memento and souvenir imaginable was on sale. On Coronation Eve, the Mall was packed 12 deep, with 30,000 people bedded down for the night in the hope of a good view on the big day. The ceremony was filmed for television for the first time. The Queen had fought a battle with some of her closest advisers, including the Earl Marshall, the Archbishop of Canterbury and Sir Winston Churchill, over this issue. She felt strongly that it was only right and natural for as many of her subjects as possible to see her Coronation.

Every day for weeks before the Coronation, the Queen practised walking down the aisle with a sheet pinned to her shoulders in imitation of her Coronation robes and rehearsed to records of her father's Coronation ceremony. She took lessons and daily readings and meditations from the Archbishop of Canterbury, Geoffrey Fisher.

The great day, 2 June, dawned grey and drizzly but the newspapers brought wonderful news. A British team led by Captain John Hunt and Edmund Hillary of New Zealand had conquered Mount Everest for the first time. After three hours of processions

44

and guests arriving at Westminster Abbey, the State Coach carrying the Queen and the Duke of Edinburgh drew up outside. After a ceremony lasting three hours, the newly crowned Queen emerged from the Abbey to meet the people and acknowledge their cheers.

When the Queen embarked on her ambitious world tour on 23 November 1953, she became the first British Sovereign to travel around the world. She visited Bermuda and Jamaica and then sailed through the Panama Canal to Fiji and Tonga, and reached New Zealand by Christmas day. The Queen saw the upholding of the ideals and unity of the Commonwealth as one of her most important responsibilities. In the first-ever Christmas broadcast to be made outside Great Britain, she spoke of her belief in this unifying role: 'I want to show that the Crown is not merely an abstract symbol of our unity, but a personal and living bond between you and me.' She was the first reigning Monarch ever to visit New Zealand. When she arrived in Australia on 3 February 1954, she told the crowds that she was addressing them not only as the Queen of Great Britain but as their national Monarch: 'I am proud indeed to be at the head of a nation that has achieved so much,' she said.

The Queen and her entourage spent two months travelling over Australia's huge terrain, covering 2500 miles by rail, 900 by car and a further 10,000 by plane. She made 102 speeches, listened to 200 more and heard the National Anthem played over 160 times. She opened the Australian Parliament wearing her wedding dress. 'It is my resolve,' she declared, 'that under God I shall not only rule but serve. This is not only the tradition of my family; it describes, I believe, the modern character of the British Crown.' She then travelled on to Ceylon and Uganda. Her children Prince Charles and Princess Anne had been staying with their great-uncle 'Dickie' Mountbatten in Malta. The whole family enjoyed a happy reunion at Tobruk, off North Africa. Back in London, a very enthusiastic reception awaited the Royal Yacht *Britannia* as she sailed up the Thames under Tower Bridge. The Queen and her party had been away for 173 days. At Southampton the Queen had been greeted by Winston Churchill, one of her proudest and most loyal subjects. A close and trusting friendship had developed between Prime Minister and Sovereign. They both enjoyed their weekly

46

LEFT An official study of Elizabeth and Philip.

ABOVE The Queen with Sir Winston Churchill, for whom she had great respect.

meetings at Buckingham Palace, when Churchill would insist on wearing a frockcoat to see the Queen. He would not forego the traditional trek to Balmoral to see the Monarch, even after suffering from two strokes in 1952. However, he was frail and in June 1954 suffered a further stroke. In traditional style he entertained his Sovereign at 10 Downing Street on the eve of his resignation on 5 April 1955.

The pattern of Queen Elizabeth's everyday life was by now well established. Bobo would bring her a tray of tea at 8 am and she would spend the morning reading letters and the newspapers, taking breakfast with her husband and seeing her children. She would telephone her mother and her sister before settling down to work at 10 am. Every morning, down the Mall from Whitehall, a little horse-drawn carriage would come clopping, bearing one of the Royal Messengers with a pile of 'the boxes' for the Queen to deal with. All political and administrative letters and requests from charities for the Queen to visit hospitals and schools and so on would be dealt with by the office staff and ladies-in-waiting. Before her afternoon engagements began, equerries and private secretaries would bring the Queen a timetable of events and a list of everyone she would be meeting that afternoon. Two Rolls-Royces would approach the garden entrance of Buckingham Palace and the Queen and Prince Philip would climb into the first car, and their attendants into the second. With the route ahead cleared by Scotland Yard, the royal visit could begin.

The Queen preferred to meet people in small groups if possible. She would usually be back at the Palace by 5 pm, ready to kick off her shoes and enjoy another cup of tea.

48

Andrew, who was followed by another boy, Prince Edward, in March 1964. The Queen's decision to enlarge her family took some royal observers by surprise, but the Queen had always intended to have a larger family than the ten-year gap between Anne and Andrew indicated. Her accession to the throne interrupted the process and now she was delighted with her new sons – she was a more-relaxed, confident mother the second time around. This trend for renewal and regeneration was continued by Princess Margaret who announced her engagement to Antony Armstrong-Jones on 25 February 1960.

They had met two years previously when Armstrong-Jones had been commissioned to take photographs of Prince Charles and Princess Anne. News of the engagement caused quite a stir in royal circles. Educated at Eton and Cambridge, where he coxed the boat crew to victory and left without taking his finals in architecture, Armstrong-Jones had a fairly colourful family history. His father was a three-times-married barrister and his mother had remarried an Irish Peer, having two more children by him. The new addition to the royal family had set himself up in business as a photographer in a studio in Pimlico and became a sought-after magazine and portrait photographer. He moved in a society far removed from the staid conventions of Buckingham Palace. Amiable, talented and deeply artistic by nature, he was a member of a very fashionable, contemporary set of artists, actors, and choreographers. Even the progressive *New Statesman* commented that his marriage to Princess Margaret had to be viewed with 'a leniency which only a few years before would have been unthinkable'. The Queen quickly grew fond of her prospective brother-in-law; they shared the same sense of humour and enjoyed the same jokes.

Princess Margaret married the newly created Lord Snowdon on the beautifully sunny day of 6 May 1960. Eighteen months later she had a son, David, Viscount

FAR LEFT *A picture of a very special grandmother, Queen Elizabeth the Queen Mother, with a rather cross looking Princess Anne and a smiling Prince Charles sticking close to his grandmother.*

ABOVE *Princess Margaret and her husband the Earl of Snowdon pose for the first formal portrait after their marriage on 6 May 1960.*

TOP *The royal family at Frogmore, Windsor. One-year-old Prince Edward is the centre of attention.*

54

ABOVE Princess Margaret
and Lord Snowdon with
their best man and flower
girls on their wedding day.

LEFT Queen Elizabeth
with Prince Andrew and
two of her famous pet
corgis at Windsor Castle.

RIGHT The Queen with
Charles and Anne in 1964.

56

ABOVE A scene from the six-month-long around the world tour of the Commonwealth in 1953. Queen Elizabeth and the Duke of Edinburgh pass under a flowery arch which reads 'Long Live The Queen' as they drive down the seventeenth-century streets of St George in Bermuda, December 1953.

ABOVE RIGHT Queen Elizabeth accepts a whale's tooth, a token of good will, from a Fijian chief after the royal tour arrives in Suva Harbour, December 1953.

RIGHT The Queen and Prince Philip on a visit to the Waitomo caves, New Zealand. The royal couple made the visit by boat down an underground river.

Linley, and almost four years to the day after the wedding, a daughter, Lady Sarah Armstrong Jones, was born. Lord Snowdon continued to work as a photographer and accompanied his wife on many of her royal visits abroad. Princess Margaret found it difficult to reconcile her royal position with her own individuality and resented her status as a modern woman living a regimented life from a bygone era.

The 1960s saw the Queen adapting to the times. She insisted on continuing her state visit to Ghana despite the unsettled political situation and regardless of personal danger. Likewise, she ignored anti-British and therefore anti-Monarchy sentiments which were running high during her visit to Canada in 1964. During the Rhodesian Crisis she sent a personal letter to Ian Smith which made it clear she did not support his position or views. On Winston Churchill's death she made the decision to honour him with a state funeral, and by her order his widow and family occupied the place of honour in the procession to St Paul's Cathedral.

The 1960s ended on a splendid high note with the Investiture of Prince Charles as Prince of Wales, at Caernavon castle in Wales on 1 July 1969. He had been the first future sovereign to take an honours degree (he studied archaeology and anthropology at Trinity College, Cambridge where his mentor was Rab Butler). He had also studied for a term at Aberystwyth University where he learnt Welsh. The Investiture was a day of simple grandeur and great pageantry. The Prince spoke fluently in Welsh as he assumed the traditional Welsh crown. As Charles swore fealty, the Queen heard the same oath spoken by her husband on the day of her Coronation: 'I, Charles, Prince of Wales, do become your liegeman of life and limb and of earthly worship; and faith and truth I will bear unto you to leave and die against all manner of folks.'

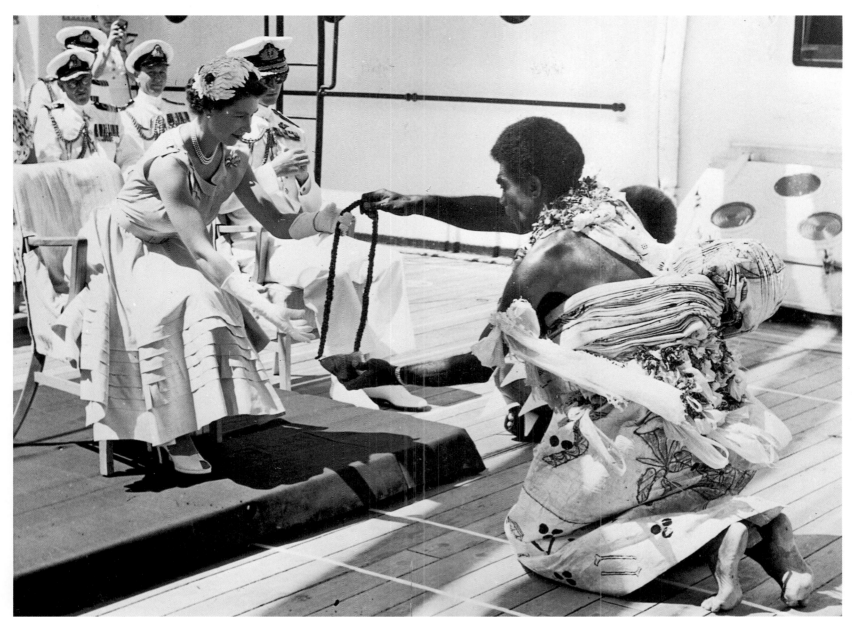

A GLORIOUS REIGN

Prince Philip has sought to establish his own identity and separate role within the monarchy. Initially, he was content to stay in the background to support, and, most importantly in his opinion, protect, his wife. He was a moving force behind the new media openness and accessibility that was instituted in the 1960s. A TV film, 'The Royal Palaces of Britain', which looked at the beauties of royal residences such as Buckingham Palace, Windsor Castle and St James's Palace, was a major step forward in royal media relations. A joint ITV/BBC production, it was first shown on Christmas Day 1966 and was a popular success, leading to a more ambitious film – a documentary about the royal family itself. *Royal Family* involved 75 days of shooting and was watched by more people worldwide than any other documentary film at that time.

The film was a revolutionary idea: viewers saw the Queen as a private family woman, driving her car, organizing barbecues, relaxing with her family and her dogs. The Queen was seen sitting on a sofa with Andrew and Edward, showing them a family album and testing them on their knowledge of their royal ancestors. Prince Philip kept a close eye on the filming to guard against encroachment upon his wife's privacy. More than once the director/producer Richard Cawston heard him shout 'don't bring your bloody cameras so close to the Queen'.

Prince Philip has become perhaps the most controversial member of the Royal Family. He likes to speak his mind and has his own very definite opinions. He is a straightforward man who appreciates the same quality in others. He has waged a one-man war against the Press and his conflicts with journalists are too numerous to

BELOW A relaxed family photo of the Queen, Prince Philip, Charles, Anne and Andrew taken at Windsor, 1962.

RIGHT A formal portrait of the Queen with Philip, Charles and Anne in the salon at Sandringham, 1970.

LEFT   A Cecil Beaton photographic portrait of the Queen, ready to bestow the Order of the Garter, in a ceremony held at St George's Chapel, Windsor in June 1956.

ABOVE   Queen Elizabeth accepts a bouquet of orchids from a young Nigerian girl in Lagos on her arrival at the Ijora power station during her tour of Africa in 1956.

TOP   Queen Elizabeth is welcomed in Lagos, Nigeria.

mention. He has provided the tabloids with excellent copy over the years – such as the occasion when he shot a tiger in India in 1961 – and his infamous speech to the captains of British industry in which he said they needed to 'pull their fingers out'.

He has followed in the footsteps of Prince Albert in his patronage of science and technology. In 1951 he was appointed President of the British Association for the Advancement of Sciences. In 1962 he even invited a team of efficiency experts to conduct a survey of how well Buckingham Palace was run. He has aligned himself with the conservationist cause, most notably in his presidency of the World Wildlife Fund, which has not been without controversy when his predilection for hunting and shooting seem to contradict his environmental concerns. The Duke of Edinburgh Award Schemes is the project most associated with his name. Set up early into the reign of the Queen, it aims to channel the energies of thousands of young people in challenging and rewarding programmes at three levels: bronze silver and gold. Every year, he invites gold level graduates of the scheme to meet him at Buckingham Palace. He does not object to exploiting his royal position in the aid of a good cause. He successfully petitioned the Chancellor of the Exchequer when he felt that the National Maritime Museum, of which he is a trustee, was not getting the funding it deserved. During a tour of the United States in 1966, the Duke was visiting Florida when a Miami Beach business man dared him to dive into a swimming pool, with the promise of an award of $100,000 to the Variety Club charities in the UK for which the Duke was raising funds. He needed no further encouragement and promptly dived in and collected the cheque.

He has settled into the role of old-fashioned *paterfamilias* with considerable ease. He is a formidable, intelligent opponent in an argument: the Queen has been known to encourage the opposition with light-hearted shouts of 'You tell him!' Prince Philip writes his own speeches; and very good they are too, uniquely his own in style and with his own salty language and humour. After-dinner speaking has become a favourite hobby. He has certainly brought authority and a cutting edge to the monarchy. No-one could ever accuse him of blandness. 'There is something valuable in people living their own style' he has said, 'I don't think people mind a little downright rudeness and prejudice. They excuse all that provided the person actually does the stuff they expect them to do.' He and the Queen are acknowledged, by those who really know them, to have a very strong and loving marriage. In November 1972 they celebrated their Silver Wedding Anniversary and after a special ceremony in Westminster Abbey to mark

62

the occasion, the Queen cleverly turned a royal cliché on its head when she joked at a Guildhall dinner: 'I think everyone will concede that today, of all occasions, I should begin my speech with "my husband and I".' The official photograph of the Queen and Prince Philip taken as part of the anniversary celebrations shows the couple smiling, relaxed, and totally at ease with each other. It is an accurate reflection of their relationship then and now.

In 1969 Prince Philip reopened the debate on the always controversial subject of the Civil List by publicly noting that the Queen's allowance had not risen for 17 years. These payments to the Royal Household are always controversial, and his act indirectly led to a Select Committee being set up to investigate the official Royal finances. After the most detailed and thorough invesitgation, in 1971 the Committee recommended an increase and that future payments should be adjusted to take account of inflation.

Of course, the Queen has a personal fortune, and indeed has been identified as the richest woman in the world and among the top ten richest people in the world by at least one survey. Her real wealth is difficult to calculate as the line between what she owns and what is in fact owned by the State is far from clear, but her exemption from tax means that her wealth has not been eroded in the post-war years.

In November 1973, Westminster Abbey was once again the setting for an important

family occasion – the marriage of Princess Anne and Captain Mark Phillips. This most modern of princesses wanted her wedding to be as informal and natural as possible. She refused to have 'hordes of uncontrollable children' attend her and picked just Prince Edward and Lady Sarah Armstrong Jones.

Princess Margaret's marriage to Lord Snowdon was sadly in difficulties in the early 1970s. The Queen suggested a reconciliation but when that seemed impossible, the

couple separated. When the Press linked Margaret's name with that of 'Roddy' Llewellyn a scandal seemed likely. Although she could not in her position as head of the Church condone a divorce, neither has the Queen condemned either party. She has tried to offer her support to both and to make the best arrangements possible for the children of the marriage. The couple formally divorced in 1976.

The Silver Jubilee year of 1977 focused attention back on the Queen, who took

LEFT A romantic yet formal official portrait of Queen Elizabeth II.

ABOVE The queen looks relaxed and happy to be indulging in one of her favourite pastimes – watching the Badminton Horse Trials in 1957. The Queen Mother is second from left in the picture. The Queen is recording the event for her own private collection.

LEFT The Queen and Philip pose on a bridge in the grounds of Buckingham Palace, looking down on Prince Charles and Princess Anne.

ABOVE Princess Margaret, Lord Snowdon and their children Sarah and David in the garden of Kensington Palace.

centre stage once more after years of her family sharing the spotlight. After a quiet start, the year built up into a tremendous display of gratitude and affection for Her Majesty.

The Jubilee tours abroad began in February and continued until the end of March and then began again from October to November, with the British celebrations in between. The Queen travelled a total of 56,000 miles. Nobody knew or felt more keenly than the Queen herself how pointless these visits were to some of the people in the more poverty stricken Commonwealth countries. The tours could be exhausting and the itinerary was demanding. As a member of the Queen's Household asked a journalist from the *Daily Telegraph* during a visit to Barbados: 'Have you ever tried smiling continuously for even 12 miles?'

During Jubilee Year, there was a renewal of affection between the British people and their Sovereign. Over 100,000 people wrote in to Buckingham Palace in praise of the Queen; 3500 letters arrived on one day alone. On 4 May 1977 both Houses of Parliament gave loyal addresses to the Queen in Westminster Hall. In offering her thanks, the Queen stressed the importance of the 'Constitutional Monarchy' and the 'basic stability of our institutions, our traditions of public service, and concern for others, our family life, and, above all, the freedom you have through the ages so fearlessly upheld.' In June, the Queen and her family attended the Silver Jubilee Thanksgiving service at St Paul's Cathedral. The service ended with a prayer that Queen Elizabeth II 'should always possess the hearts of her people.'

ABOVE RIGHT Harold Macmillan addresses the crowds at the dedication of the John F Kennedy Memorial, Runnymede. Front right are Prince Philip, Queen Elizabeth, Jacqueline Kennedy and Macmillan. Robert F Kennedy is behind Jacqueline.

RIGHT The Queen with all her immediate family at Windsor, 1968.

68

ABOVE *A photograph which captures something of the essence of the relationship between the Queen and her daughter* Princess Anne, with the jodpurs, the boat, Anne's confident stance and the ever-present corgi who just sneaks into the picture.

RIGHT *Prince Andrew's debut in front of the cameras at one month old.* His mother holds him for a photograph taken by Cecil Beaton in March 1960.

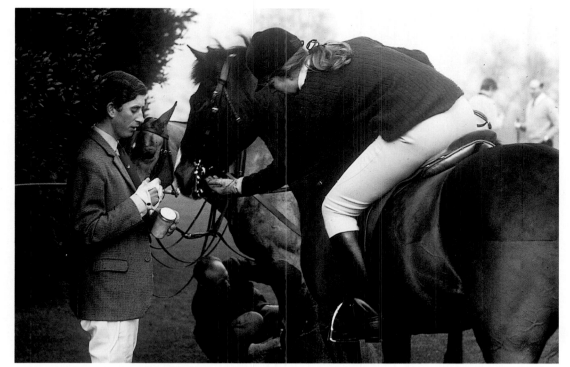

LEFT   Queen Elizabeth II and Prince Philip (dressed in the full uniform of an Admiral of the Fleet) at Buckingham Palace with their four children in 1968.

BELOW LEFT   Prince Charles takes his youngest brother Prince Edward out for a spin in a go-kart at Windsor in May 1969.

LEFT   Prince Charles and Princess Anne both enjoyed horse riding as children although his horsemanship is now mainly confined to playing polo, while Princess Anne went on to become a top international three-day eventer, competing in the Olympic games in Montreal 1976. Here they are together at Windsor, in May 1969.

ABOVE   Queen Elizabeth presents her eldest son with the sceptre after his Investiture as Prince of Wales at Caernavon Castle in July 1969. Prince Philip is seated behind them on the dais and the Home Secretary James Callaghan is among those who can be seen watching the ceremony.

In 1977, Prince Charles left the Royal Navy to head the Silver Jubilee Trust which aimed to 'help young people help themselves'. The whole country joined in the fun; there were carnivals, youth festivals, regattas, pop galas, concerts, plays, bicycle and boat races, exhibitions of everything from stamps to the Queen's Pictures and, of course, the famous street parties. The films *Royal* and *The Queen's Gardens* showed the Queen as being receptive to good advice and needful of change. Queen Elizabeth II emerged from the festivities of 1977 with a new-found confidence and authority. When she was just a girl of 16 Lady Airlie wrote of the then Princess Elizabeth: 'Although she was perfectly simple, modest and unselfconscious, she gave the impression of great personality' and this 'great personality' was refined and consolidated during her Silver Jubilee Year.

The next great royal occasion was the much feted wedding of the Prince of Wales to Lady Diana Spencer on 29 July 1981. Among all the years of speculation as to who Prince Charles would marry, no one expected him to wed the girl next door. Diana's

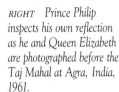

ABOVE Princess Margaret looking every inch the beautiful bride as she arrives at Westminster Abbey in the Glass Coach for her marriage to Lord Snowdon on 6 May 1960.

RIGHT Prince Philip inspects his own reflection as he and Queen Elizabeth are photographed before the Taj Mahal at Agra, India, 1961.

BELOW Queen Elizabeth II, dressed in an appropriate black lace dress and veil, has an historic meeting with Pope John XXIII in the Vatican City, Rome, 5 May 1961.

72

FAR RIGHT John F Kennedy and Queen Elizabeth II smile graciously as they are photographed at Buckingham Palace after dinner on 5 June 1961. Kennedy was the first United States President to dine there since 1918.

family home Park House was less than half a mile from Sandringham. Just 20 years old when she married the 32-year-old Prince, beautiful and the possessor of a perfect pedigree (she was a direct descendent of Charles II), she was the perfect choice. If Diana had not come along when she did, they would have had to invent her. The Queen was very pleased at the match and 'Shy Di' was soon a national celebrity. No one could have guessed that she would become a media superstar with a very high public profile. Diana was just the injection of fresh, youthful glamour combined with a touching quality of ordinariness that the royal family needed. With the birth of her two sons Prince William and Prince Harry, and her dedication to work and duty, she has more than fulfilled what was expected of her.

Like her father and grandfather, Queen Elizabeth II is happiest in the country. Horses were her first love. She had dozens of toy horses to play with as a small child and loved to ride her pony over the moors of Balmoral when she was able. It was not until 1949 that she became directly involved in horseracing, when she and her mother bought Monaveen, a steeplechaser. Monaveen enjoyed a good career until a fall at the Hurst Park water jump ended her life and Princess Elizabeth's interest in steeplechasing. She decided to concentrate solely on the flat and in 1952 bought Aureole, a two-year-old chestnut colt and son of Hyperion, the legendary stallion of the 1930s. As a three-year-old, Aureole was expected to win the Epsom Derby for the Queen in the year of her coronation, but Gordon Richards won it on Pinza. Richards, who was later knighted by the Queen, said she was a 'marvellous sport' in defeat. Aureole was then defeated in the King George VI and Queen Elizabeth stakes, and the St Ledger.

After a change in jockey and some neurological treatment to help calm his temperament, Aureole came good in 1954, winning the Hardwicke Stakes at Ascot and the George VI and Queen Elizabeth Stakes. He helped the Queen become the most successful owner that year. The Queen's next racing successes came with fillies. Mulberry

LEFT Princess Anne and Captain Mark Phillips leave the altar in Westminster Abbey after their marriage.

ABOVE The happy couple with page boy and bridesmaid.

Harbour, bred at Sandringham, won the French Derby in 1957 and the Cheshire and Newmarket Oaks. When Lester Piggot rode Carozza to victory at the Epsom Oaks, it gave the Queen the first-ever royal victory in a race that was founded in the eighteenth century. Her greatest filly of the 1950s was Almeria, who became the country's best three-year-old filly by winning at Royal Ascot, Goodwood, York and Doncaster. The 1960s were a poorer decade for the Queen's horses but the 1970s and 1980s brought more triumphs. Dunfermline won the Epsom Oaks for the Queen in her Silver Jubilee Year. So far the Derby is the only major classic to have eluded her.

In 1986 the Queen celebrated her sixtieth birthday; Prince Andrew took the official photograph to commemorate the occasion. It was also the year of Andrew's engagement and marriage to the vivacious Sarah Ferguson, popularly known as 'Fergie'. The wedding at Westminster Abbey was a 'family' affair. Their daughters Beatrice and Eugenie were born in 1988 and 1990 respectively. On a rather less happy note, Princess Anne announced her separation from Mark Philips in 1990 amid some acrimony.

LEFT *Queen Elizabeth and Prince Philip, wearing the uniform of the Grenadier Guards and the ceremonial uniform of a Field Marshal respectively, 'take the salute' of mounted troops passing in review in front of Buckingham Palace after their return from the Trooping of the Colour on 11 June 1953. This ceremony, which is over two-hundred-years old, marks the official birthday of the Queen every year.*

RIGHT *This much more contemporary-style photograph of Queen Elizabeth and Prince Philip shows them at ease in natural surroundings. Taken at Balmoral, Scotland in October 1972, the photograph was released to commemorate the Queen's silver wedding anniversary on 20 November 1972.*

BELOW *This formal photograph of Prince Philip and the Queen, taken in the Long Gallery of Windsor Castle in 1976, still tells us something of their private relationship as those warm, generous smiles are obviously genuine.*

It is fortunate indeed that Queen Elizabeth II, who was not born to be Queen, has proved to be so ideally suited to her role. Her intelligence, humour, compassion and pragmatic nature have allowed her to fulfill her aim of representing the spirit of the national character at home and abroad. She is the United Kingdom's greatest ambassador. Her reign has been one of great change. British influence and prestige abroad have diminished but the esteem in which the British Monarchy is held has risen, thanks to the hard work and dedication of the Sovereign.

In the political sphere, she has been faultless. When Harold Wilson retired in 1976 he said of her: 'I shall certainly advise my successor to do his homework before his audience and to read all his telegrams and Cabinet Committee papers in time . . . or he will feel like an unprepared schoolboy.' Harold MacMillan wrote that the Queen's grasp of details was 'astonishing' and Edward Heath remembered that the Queen always achieved the delicate task of listening and encouraging without ever interfering and said 'the fact that she has all these years of experience and is so imperturbable is a source of encouragement in itself.' Unlike her mother, the Queen saw the loss of the colonies as inevitable in the long run, for she is a realistic, progressively minded woman.

It has been rumoured that the Queen's relationship with Britain's first woman Prime Minister, Margaret Thatcher, had been stormy, but other reporters suggest that they had the business-like approach to be expected from two such independent women. As in so many instances, it is difficult to separate speculation from fact.

78

ABOVE Queen Elizabeth II in formal evening attire.

RIGHT The Queen and Prince Philip sorting cables of congratulation on their silver wedding anniversary, 1972.

ABOVE RIGHT The Queen photographing Princess Anne at the horse-trials.

RIGHT A photo to commemorate the royal silver wedding. Back row, standing, left to right: The Earl of Snowdon; The Duke of Kent; Prince William of Kent; The Duke of Edinburgh; The Earl of St Andrews (elder son of The Duke of Kent); Prince Charles, The Prince of Wales; Prince Andrew, Hon Angus Ogilvy and (extreme right) his son, James Ogilvy. Seated on chairs, left to right: Princess Margaret, Countess of Snowdon; The Duchess of Kent (holding Lord Nicholas Windsor, her younger son); Queen Elizabeth The Queen Mother; Queen Elizabeth II; Princess Anne; Marina Ogilvy, and her mother, Princess Alexandra. Seated on floor, left to right: Lady Sarah Armstrong-Jones, Viscount Linley (the children of Princess Margaret); Prince Edward; Lady Helen Windsor (daughter of The Duke of Kent).

Her humour and wit are perhaps her least appreciated quality. She once asked one of Prince Charles's girlfriends who had come to lunch at Windsor Castle, 'Did you find it all right?'

When the Queen Mother, recovering from an illness, announced that she had every intention of living to be a hundred, the Queen replied 'Then it'll be Charles who'll send you your centenarian telegram.' Of all the tributes paid to the Queen over the years none is more pertinent than the love and respect her subjects have for her. In an age when royalty has to prove itself to the people and where loyalty has to be earned and not taken for granted, Queen Elizabeth II has strengthened the Monarchy through her strength as an individual. When the Prince and Princess of Wales left St Paul's Cathedral after their wedding in July 1981, a golden banner proclaimed these hopeful words: 'All shall be well, and all manner of things shall be well.' Nothing would please the Queen more than that these words held true for the state of the British Monarchy long into the future.

80

ABOVE *The Queen poses with Yeomen of the Guard, 1974.*

ABOVE RIGHT *An informal view of the Queen while at the Marathon Coaching Event at the Royal Windsor Horse Show in which Philip is participating, 1973.*

RIGHT *The Queen with her immediate family including Captain Mark Phillips in 1976.*

OVERLEAF *Queen Elizabeth arriving at Ascot on Ladies' Day.*

RIGHT Prince Andrew points to the crowd as thousands of children, gathered in front of Buckingham Palace, sing for the Queen on her sixtieth birthday on 21 April 1986. The Prince's fiancée Sarah 'Fergie' Ferguson can be seen on his left, enjoying her first official royal 'event'.

BELOW Queen Elizabeth II and Prince Philip in the Chamber of the House of Lords, January 1989.

84

RIGHT The Queen
dressed in her red and white
ceremonial robes for the
Order of the Bath
Ceremony, 1982.

BELOW RIGHT The
Queen pictured with (left
to right) the Duchess of
York, Prince Charles,
Princess Diana, and the
Queen Mother at the
Braemar Games, Scotland,
1986.

LEFT The Braemar Games have been a regular outing for the royal family during their holidays at Balmoral. Here the Queen is accompanied by Prince Philip and her sons Andrew and Edward.

88

ABOVE The Queen looks warm and cheerful in a fur hat and brightly coloured outfit. Sometimes criticized for her dress sense, the Queen is not one to pander to the received wisdom of fashion commentators.

RIGHT The Queen engaged in a walkabout (the term first came into use during her reign and is now very much part of royal public life), during her Silver Jubilee year of 1977, a year of fun and celebration which more than answered the doubters who wondered whether the monarchy was still relevant or popular in modern Britian.

LEFT Prince Charles and Princess Diana descend the steps of St Paul's Cathedral on their wedding day.

LEFT The Queen and Prince Philip in an open landau on their way to Ascot.

BELOW One of the most famous kisses in modern history: Prince Charles kisses his lovely bride, the Princess of Wales on their wedding day on 29 July 1981.

ABOVE Diana, Princess of Wales, holds the infant Prince William during the photo session at his christening in Buckingham Palace in August 1982. Other members of the royal family present in the photograph are (from left to right) standing, Prince Charles, Prince Philip, and seated the Queen, and the Queen Mother.

RIGHT The Queen, veiled and in black, waits to meet Pope John Paul II at the Vatican in 1980.

RIGHT Dressed in their warm winter coats, the royal family attend church at Sandringham in December 1985.

BELOW Prince William at Sandringham, 1988.

BELOW The Queen's relationship with her Prime Minister Margaret Thatcher caused much conjecture in the press (most of it unsubstantiated). They are seen together at the Commonwealth Conference in 1979.

94

LEFT The Queen sits among the heads of Governments for the group photograph at the Commonwealth Conference in Lusaka, Zambia, in 1979.

BELOW LEFT The Queen inspects the Royal 22nd Regiment during a visit to the Citadel, Quebec City, Canada in October 1982.

RIGHT The Queen shakes hands with Benazir Bhutto on board the royal yacht Britannia before the start of a dinner hosted by Her Majesty for the Commonwealth heads of Government in Kuala Lumpur, Malaysia, in October 1989.

BELOW A Maori canoe passes in front of Queen Elizabeth's barge as she arrives in Waitanga, New Zealand, 1990.

LEFT Her Majesty Queen Elizabeth II takes the salute at the Trooping of the Colour.

RIGHT Prince Charles kisses his mother's hand after a polo match in Windsor Great Park.

BELOW The Queen, in jubilant pose, at the Derby race meeting of 1988. Prince and Princess Michael of Kent are pictured with her.

LEFT The Queen and
Prince Philip visit the Great
Wall on their tour of
China.

TOP The Queen arrives
for an official visit to
Jordan in 1984.

ABOVE The Queen
accepts a bouquet as she
strolls in the Queen's
Gardens, Sydney, 1986.

LEFT Prince Andrew and his wife Sarah, the Duchess of York, have their turn kissing on the balcony of Buckingham Palace after their wedding on 23 July 1986.

RIGHT Britain's most glamorous royal superstar, the Princess of Wales, steps out with Prince Charles at the National Gallery, Washington DC, in 1986.

BELOW The Queen and Prince Philip with the Queen Mother and Princess Anne at the funeral of the Duchess of Windsor, St George's Chapel, Windsor in 1986.

102

ABOVE Four generations of the royal family are pictured together at the christening of Prince Harry. Left to right are the Queen Mother; Queen Elizabeth; the Princess of Wales holding Prince Henry, and Prince Charles.

RIGHT Princess Diana in a low-cut velvet evening gown at the premiere of Back to the Future in 1985.

RIGHT Mother and daughter, in contrasting blue and scarlet at Windsor Great Park in 1986.

OVERLEAF The Queen makes an historic address to the United States Congress in May 1991.

ABOVE LEFT The Queen and the royal family on the balcony of Buckingham Palace for the Trooping of the Colour ceremony in 1988.

LEFT The Queen poses for a photograph with the Royal Welsh Fusiliers Regiment in April 1989.

ABOVE Queen Elizabeth II in a relaxed mood for a photographic portrait in 1985.

LEFT Prince Charles
playing polo at West Palm
Beach during his visit to
Florida in 1988.

ABOVE Prince Charles
looks down on Prince
William and Prince Harry
as they snuggle up to mum
on a holiday with King
Juan Carlos of Spain in
Palma de Mallorca, in
Spain.

LEFT   The Queen Mother and her closest relatives gather outside Clarence House on her ninetieth birthday in August 1990.

LEFT   The Queen in a jaunty hat and an emerald green outfit for the Gulf War parade at Petersfield in 1991.

BELOW LEFT   A crowd gathers in front of Buckingham Palace to enjoy their celebrations of the Queen's sixtieth birthday in April 1986.

BELOW   Queen Elizabeth II chats with Prince Andrew and the Duchess of York aboard HMS Campbeltown (the Prince's ship) in 1991.

ACKNOWLEDGMENTS

The publisher would like to thank Sue Rose, the designer, Kathy Schneider for picture research and the agencies and individuals listed below for supplying the photographs:

Marcus Adams/Camera Press/Globe Photos: pp 21; Baron/Camera Press/Globe Photos: pp 37; Cecil Beaton/Camera Press/Globe/Globe Photos: pp 1, 41, 55, 69; Bettmann Newsphotos: pp 9, 11, 13 (both), 18, 28 (top), 31 (bottom), 33 (bottom left), 34, 44 (top left), 46, 47, 61 (bottom), 64, 85 (bottom), 93 (bottom left), 99 (top), 100 (bottom), 102 (bottom), 103; Bettmann Newsphotos/Hulton: pp 4-5, 12, 14 (left), 15 (top), 17 (bottom), 25 (both), 26 (right), 27, 28 (bottom), 29 (both), 30, 39, 44 (bottom), 45, 75; BPL; pp 49 (bottom); Camera Press/Globe: pp 7, 10, 40, 51 Anwar Hussein: pp 15 (bottom), 50 (bottom), 81 (bottom), 82-3, 85 (top), 86-7, 88, 89, 92 (bottom), 93 (top and bottom right), 94 (top), 96, 97 (both), 98, 104-5, 106 (both), 110 (both), 111 (both); Illustrated London News: pp 19 (right), 20 (both); Imperial War Museum: pp 33 (bottom right); Reuters/Bettmann Newsphotos: pp 84 (top), 94 (bottom), 95 (both), 99 (bottom), 100 (top), 102 (top), 107, 108, 109; John Scott: pp 90; S&G Press Agency: pp 38 (main pic); UBI/Bettmann Newsphotos: pp 2, 6, 8 (both), 14 (right), 16, 17 (top), 22, 23, 24 (both), 26 (left), 31 (top), 32, 33 (top, both), 35, 36, 38 (inset), 42, 43, 44 (top right), 48, 49 (top), 52, 53 (both), 54 (both), 56, 57 (both), 58, 59, 60, 61 (top), 62, 63, 65 (both), 66, 67, 68, 70 (both), 71 (both), 72 (all 3), 73, 74, 76, 77 (both), 78 (both), 79 (both), 80, 81 (top), 84 (bottom), 91 (both), 92 (top), 101; Weidenfeld & Nicolson Archives: pp 50 (top);